Fat, Fiber, & Low Sugar CookBook

Give The Low Sugar High Fiber Diet a Chance

40 Delicious & Healthy Recipes That Your Family Will Love

by

New Health CookBooks

COPYRIGHT

DISCLAIMER

New Health CookBooks

Contents

Preface   ix
Chapter 1: Breakfast   1
Pizza-For-Breakfast Strata   2
Banana-Berry Irish Oats   4
Fresh Fruit Salad   5
Apple Pie Wheat Cereal   6
Quick Egg-Spinach Wraps   7
Incredibly Fast Egg Bowls   9
Cheesy Crustless Quiche   10
Bacon-Chili Skillet Frittata   12
Chapter 2: Lunches   15
Southwest Chicken Wrap   16
Ham & Cheese Egg Salad Sandwiches   18
Springtime Sandwich Wraps   19
Blue Cheese Barley   21
Smoky-Sweet Baked Potatoes   22
Chicken Salad with Fruit   24
Tex-Mex Chicken Lettuce Wraps   25
Italian Patty Melts   26
Chapter 3: Dinners   29
Hearty Main Dish Greek Salad   30
Garlic Tofu Stir-Fry   32
Vegetable Frittata   34
Chicken-Stuffed Mediterranean   36
Greek Chicken Tabbouleh   38
Pesto Salmon with Green Beans   40
Chicken Wild Rice Soup/Vegetables   42

New Health CookBooks

Contents

Pizza Casserole   44

Cheesy Chicken-Quinoa Bake   46

Taco Skillet   48

Greek Spaghetti Squash   50

Vegetable-Burger Stir Fry   52

Hearty Steak and Cauliflower   54

Quick-Cooking Italian Chicken   56

Roasted Pork Chop Supper   58

Chicken-Bulgur Florentine   60

Herb-Seasoned Tomato-Chicken   62

Chapter 4: Snacks   65

Grab-and-Go Tropical Trail Mix   66

Cajun Spiced Popcorn   67

Southwest Toasted Pepitas   68

Savory Stuffed Mushrooms   71

Classic Buffalo Wings   72

Creamy Deviled Eggs   74

Coco-Nutty Banana Bites   76

Chapter 5 Additional Resources   77

Popular Best Selling CookBooks   78

Weight Loss and Diet Books   82

Preface

In this helpful cookbook, you will find 40 delicious recipes that are low-sugar and high in fiber, perfect for those following the Fat Chance program. Many recipes include ingredients that contain high levels of healthy fats, while avoiding trans-fats and omega-6 fats. Don't worry--as many of the health experts have explained, the Low-Fat, High Carb message that has been preached since the 70's is simply bad medicine.

If you have not yet read the book Fat Chance or Fat Chance Cookbook by Robert H. Lustig, we highly recommend that you read both so that you will understand why we have carefully designed these recipes with very specific ingredients. We have placed a link to it below for your convenience, and can not emphasize enough how life changing Dr. Lustig's books will be for your health.

Fiber is the other game changer when it comes to regulating insulin levels, and most of the recipes in this book include the types of fiber that will help you lose weight, lessen the effects of diabetes, and promote overall health.

We hope you love these recipes as much as we do, and experience the improved energy levels, weight loss, and overall better health that are a result of better food choices.

Now here's how to find Fat Chance and Fat Chance Cookbook by Dr. Robert Lustig. Be sure to read them so that you understand why these recipes are so effective. Just search your favorite book store for

Fat Chance by Dr. Robert H. Lustig, M.D.
Fat Chance Cookbook by Dr. Robert H. Lustig, M.D.

Enjoy!

Chapter 1

Breakfast

Pizza-For-Breakfast Strata

Instead of nitrite-packed sausage and white bread, this easy, make-ahead strata uses healthy meats and hearty whole grains. Whole grains breads are acceptable up to 5 times per week. **Serves: 12**

Ingredients:

1 pound organic, grass fed and/or free range ground chicken, pork or beef

1 tablespoon salt-free Italian seasoning blend

1 pound whole-grain bread, cubed

8 ounces fresh button mushrooms, washed and sliced

1/4 cup diced green onions

1/2 cup chopped red bell pepper

1/2 cup chopped green bell pepper

10 eggs, whipped lightly

3 cups half-and-half

1 teaspoon dried mustard

1/4 teaspoon salt

1 cup shredded mozzarella cheese

To Prepare:

Grease a 13x9 inch baking dish; scatter bread cubes in dish. In a large skillet, cook ground meat, Italian seasoning and mushrooms until meat is cooked through and mushrooms are browned; drain. Layer meat mixture and green onions on top of bread cubes in pan.
In a large bowl, lightly beat eggs. Using a whisk, combine eggs with half-and-half, mustard and salt. Pour this mixture over meat and bread in pan; sprinkle cheese on top.
Cover with plastic wrap and refrigerate overnight.

To Bake:

Remove strata from refrigerator 30 minutes before baking. Bake at 350 degrees for 60 to 70 minutes, or until a knife inserted in the center of strata comes out clean. Let strata stand for 10 minutes prior to serving. If your strata is browning too quickly, tent the pan with foil.
Notes:
Unbaked strata can be frozen for up to 3 months. To prepare, thaw in the refrigerator overnight, remove and let sit at room temperature for 30 minutes, and then bake as directed.
Pre-shredded Italian cheese blends can be used instead of mozzarella for even more flavor.

Banana-Berry Irish Oats

Irish oats, also known as steel-cut oats, take a bit longer to cook. The whole-grain health benefits, however, are well worth the extra effort. **Serves: 4**

Ingredients:

1 cup Irish (steel cut) oats

3 cups water

2 ripe bananas, sliced

1 cup fresh, washed, sliced strawberries

3/4 cup heavy cream or half-and-half

1 cup toasted pecans, chopped

Apple pie spice

To Prepare:

Combine the oats and water in a saucepan. Bring to a boil and partially cover. Reduce heat and simmer, stirring occasionally, until oats reach desired consistency (between 20 and 30 minutes).

To Serve:

Portion oats into bowls; divide bananas, strawberries, cream and pecans between each bowl as desired. Sprinkle with apple pie spice to taste.

Fresh Fruit Salad

A great addition to any holiday breakfast spread, be sure to serve this sweet salad alongside plenty of protein and fiber for a balanced start to your day! **Serves: 8**

Ingredients:

1/2 cup sour cream

2 tablespoons raw honey (see note)

1 tablespoon fresh lime juice

1/4 teaspoon fresh lime zest

1 cup fresh organic blueberries

4 fresh organic kiwis, peeled and sliced

3 sweet oranges, peeled and quartered

3 cups sliced fresh organic strawberries

1 cup seedless organic white grapes

1/4 cup chopped fresh mint leaves

To Prepare:

Thoroughly combine sour cream and honey. In a large bowl, combine all remaining ingredients. Add sour cream mixture and toss to coat.

Note:

Due to the potential presence of bacteria, small children should not be given raw honey.

Apple Pie Wheat Cereal

Capturing the flavors of everybody's favorite fruit pie, this simple, speedy breakfast will keep you energized all morning! **Serves: 4**

Ingredients:

4 cups unsweetened bite-size wheat-biscuit cereal OR 8 large wheat-cereal biscuits

2 cups milk

1 cup unsweetened Greek yogurt

1/4 cup golden raisins

1 teaspoon cinnamon

1/2 teaspoon nutmeg

1/2 teaspoon ground ginger

To Prepare:

Working in individual bowls, microwave 1 cup of bite-size OR 2 large biscuits cereal with 1/2 cup milk for 20 seconds on high. Stir; cook another 20 seconds. Repeat with remaining servings. Evenly divide yogurt, raisins, cinnamon, nutmeg and ginger between each bowl.

Note:

For an even creamier version, serve heavy (whipping) cream or half-and-half with cereal; let each diner add as desired.

Quick Egg-Spinach Wraps

Great for busy mornings, this recipe uses minimally-processed whole-wheat tortillas, which are acceptable 3 to 5 times per week.
Serves: 4

Ingredients:

8 organic, cage-free eggs

1/2 cup organic milk

2 tablespoons butter

Sea salt and freshly cracked black pepper to taste

4 whole-wheat tortillas

1 (10 ounce) bag baby spinach leaves, washed and patted dry

1 cup shredded cheddar cheese

To Prepare:

In a bowl, combine eggs and milk. Combine, then whisk until fluffy.
In a large, nonstick skillet over medium-low heat, melt butter. Add eggs and cook, stirring as needed, until cooked through. Remove from heat.

To Serve:

Divide eggs evenly between each tortilla; top with baby spinach leaves and shredded cheese. Fold ends up and roll to create a pocket.

Incredibly Fast Egg Bowls

Stuck for time in the morning? You can still enjoy a hearty egg breakfast using your microwave! **Serves: 1**

Ingredients:

2 organic, cage-free eggs

Sea salt and freshly cracked black pepper to taste

2 tablespoons organic milk

Optional: snipped fresh chives, garlic powder

To Prepare:

Combine eggs and milk in a microwave-safe bowl. Cook on high for 1 minute, 30 seconds, stirring halfway through, or until eggs are thoroughly cooked. Season to taste with salt and pepper and, if desired, top with snipped chives and a dash of garlic powder.

Cheesy Crustless Quiche

Not only is a traditional quiche crust a hassle, but it contains unhealthy refined grains. This version delivers big taste with less work – a win-win! Turkey bacon is minimally processed and acceptable 3 to 5 times per week. **Serves: 12**

Ingredients:

5 fresh green onions, sliced

1 fresh medium tomato, chopped

12 slices turkey bacon

12 organic, cage-free eggs

1/3 cup sour cream

1 (10 ounce) package frozen chopped spinach, thawed and drained

1 cup shredded mozzarella cheese

1 cup shredded cheddar cheese

Additional fresh chopped tomato and green onions

To Prepare:

Preheat your oven to 325 degrees; grease a 13x9 inch baking dish.

In a large skillet, crisply cook bacon. Remove and drain on paper towels. Reserve 1 tablespoon bacon drippings.

In bacon drippings, sauté the mushrooms until golden brown and tender, approximately 2 minutes.

Crumble the bacon and return to pan along with tomatoes and onions; mix well. Set aside.

In a large bowl, thoroughly combine eggs and sour cream. Stir in spinach until combined. Pour into prepared baking dish.

Top eggs with both cheeses and bacon mixture; bake at 325 degrees until center is firm and eggs are cooked through. Before serving, allow quiche to stand for 5 minutes. If desired, sprinkle with additional tomato and green onions.

Bacon-Chili Skillet Frittata

With minimally-processed turkey bacon and zesty southwest flavor, this easy frittata is a great weekend breakfast treat. **Serves: 6**

Ingredients:

6 organic, cage-free eggs

1/2 cup cream cheese, softened

1 teaspoon canola oil

1/2 cup chopped red bell pepper

1/2 cup chopped green bell pepper

3 tablespoons fresh cilantro, chopped

6 slices turkey bacon, cooked crisp and crumbled

1/2 teaspoon cumin

1/2 teaspoon smoked paprika

1 teaspoon chili powder

1 cup shredded cheddar cheese, divided

To Prepare:

Preheat your oven to 400 degrees.

In an oven-proof skillet over medium heat, sauté peppers in oil until crisp-tender.

Thoroughly combine eggs and cream cheese in a bowl. Add the bacon, cilantro, seasonings and 3/4 cup cheddar cheese; combine well.

Pour mixture into skillet with peppers. Reduce heat to low and cover; cook 6 minutes or until nearly set in center.

Remove lid and place skillet in oven.

Bake for 5 minutes or until eggs are cooked through and center is set. Sprinkle with cheese; return to oven for 1 minute to melt.

Chapter 2

Lunch

Southwest Chicken Wrap

Whole-wheat tortillas are minimally processed, making them fine choices 3 to 5 times per week. You can replace the tortillas in this recipe with large lettuce leaves for a no-carb option. **Serves: 4**

Ingredients:

5 medium organic tomatoes, seeded, chopped small

1 jalapeno pepper, seeded, chopped fine

3 cups cooked free-range chicken, shredded

1 medium avocado, pitted

2 tablespoons fresh cilantro, chopped

1/4 cup salsa (no sugar added)

2 tablespoons unsweetened Greek yogurt

1 cup shredded red cabbage

1/2 cup shredded pepper-jack cheese

8 whole-wheat tortillas

To Prepare:

Thoroughly combine tomatoes, jalapeno and chicken. In a small bowl, mash avocado with cilantro, salsa and Greek yogurt.

To Serve:

Evenly divide spread between each tortilla. Top with cabbage, then tomato-chicken mixture and shredded cheese. Fold one end of tortilla under and roll up to create a portable wrap.

Note:
These wraps can easily be prepared the night before for a grab-and-go lunch option. Prepare the chicken and avocado mixtures separately and refrigerate; assemble wraps in the morning to prevent soggy tortillas.

Ham & Cheese Egg Salad Sandwiches

While minimally processed, ham and whole-grain breads are acceptable options 3 to 5 times per week. **Serves: 4**

Ingredients:

6 hard-boiled free-range eggs, peeled and chopped

1/4 cup unsweetened Greek yogurt

3/4 cup cooked ham, chopped

2 tablespoons chopped fresh chives

2 tablespoons chopped fresh green onions

1/8 teaspoon smoked paprika

1/8 teaspoon dried mustard

Freshly cracked black pepper to taste

8 slices whole-grain rye bread, toasted

To Prepare:

Combine all ingredients in a bowl; keep refrigerated. To serve, spread on 4 slices of toasted bread. Top with remaining slices.

Note:
Like all sandwiches, this can be made carb-free by omitting the bread and rolling the salad up into lettuce-leaf rolls.

Springtime Sandwich Wraps

Hearty whole-grain breads are acceptable 3 to 5 times per week. Feel free to substitute a whole grain bread for the lettuce wraps in this recipe. **Serves: 4**

Ingredients:

8 tablespoons cream cheese

4 large, sturdy leaves organic lettuce

2 cups organic carrots, shredded

2 medium-sized zucchini, organic, thinly sliced

2 cups organic arugula, washed and dried

1/4 cup fresh scallions, chopped

4 slices fresh tomato

1/3 cup purchased no-sugar-added Italian salad dressing

To Prepare:

Spread the cream cheese onto each large lettuce leaf. Build your sandwich, stacking shredded carrots, zucchini slices, arugula, tomato slices and scallions.

Drizzle dressing over each sandwich. Fold and roll each lettuce leaf to form a packet.

Blue Cheese Barley

Great for a warm-you-up winter lunch, this hearty dish depends on high-quality blue cheese for outstanding flavor. **Serves: 8**

Ingredients:

8 cups hot cooked coarse barley

1/2 cup butter

8 fresh green onions, sliced

6 ounces high-quality blue cheese, crumbled

8 ounces sour cream (organic)

To Prepare:

In a large skillet over medium heat, melt butter. Add onions and cook, stirring frequently, 7 minutes.

Reduce heat to low; stir in blue cheese and cook, stirring constantly, until cheese has melted. Remove from heat. Stir sour cream into blue cheese sauce, stirring until smooth and combined.

In a large serving bowl, toss cooked barley with sour cream-blue cheese sauce until thoroughly coated. Serve immediately.

Smoky-Sweet Baked Potatoes

A great alternative to white potatoes, these flavor-packed sweet spuds make an ideal light lunch. Turkey bacon is minimally processed and acceptable 3 to 5 times per week. **Serves: 6**

Ingredients:

6 large organic sweet potatoes, washed and scrubbed

1 tablespoon butter

1 medium red onion, thinly sliced

6 tablespoons butter

1/2 teaspoon sea salt

1/2 teaspoon freshly cracked black pepper

1/2 teaspoon smoked paprika

1 cup sour cream

3 strips turkey bacon, cooked crisp and crumbled

To Prepare:

Preheat your oven to 400 degrees.

Using a fork, pierce each potato several times for steam venting. Place the potatoes on a baking sheet and cook for 45 minutes or until tender.

Meanwhile, in a skillet over medium heat, sauté onions in 1 tablespoon butter until tender.

Once the potatoes are cool enough to handle safely but still hot, cut open the tops.

Place 1 tablespoon of butter into each potato. Top with salt, pepper, paprika, sour cream and bacon crumbles.

Note:

Potatoes can also be cooked in the microwave; this will yield a softer-skinned baked potato. Prepare as directed and, working in batches, place 2 potatoes in a microwave-safe dish.

Cook on high, turning and flipping halfway through, for approximately 15 minutes or until tender. Repeat with remaining potatoes.

Chicken Salad with Fruit

Fast and refreshing, this sweet chicken salad is great for relaxed weekend brunch or lunch. **Serves: 8**

Ingredients:

4 ounces cream cheese, at room temperature

1/2 cup Greek yogurt, unsweetened

3 cups cooked, shredded chicken, organic, free-range

1 cup peeled, cubed apples

1 cup cantaloupe, cubed

1 cup sliced fresh strawberries

1 cup celery, chopped

1/4 teaspoon sea salt

1/4 cup blanched almonds, chopped

8 cups mixed baby salad greens, organic, washed

To Prepare:

Combine all ingredients except almonds and greens.
Arrange greens on individual plates, top with chicken salad
and finish with a sprinkling of almonds.

Tex-Mex Chicken Lettuce Wraps

Melted pepper-jack over boneless chicken breasts covered in salsa... yes please! **Serves: 6**

Ingredients:

6 organic, cage-free chicken breasts halves, boneless, skinless (approximately 1 1/2 pounds)

1 tablespoon canola oil

1/3 cup no-sugar-added salsa

6 (1-ounce) slices pepper-jack cheese

1/3 cup Greek yogurt

6 large, sturdy lettuce leaves

To Prepare:

In a large skillet over medium heat, sauté chicken breast halves in oil for approximately 7 minutes per side or until no pink remains (chicken should register 165 degrees on an instant-read meat thermometer).

Spoon salsa over chicken while still in skillet; place 1 slice cheese over each breast half. Cover the skillet and let stand for 2 minutes or until cheese has melted.

Spread each lettuce leaf with Greek yogurt; place 1 topped chicken breast on each leaf and roll up.

Italian Patty Melts

For a change of pace, these patty melts can be made with any organic, free-range ground meat such as bison, turkey or chicken. **Serves: 2**

Ingredients:

1/4 cup homemade Italian salad dressing (made with olive or canola oil)

1 large red onion, sliced thinly

1 pound organic, free-range ground beef

4 (1-ounce) slices mozzarella cheese

4 cups baby spinach leaves, washed and patted dry

To Prepare:

Shape ground beef into four patties.

In a skillet over medium heat, sauté onions in salad dressing until tender, approximately 7 minutes.

In a second skillet, cook patties over medium heat until cooked through (see note).

Top each with a slice of cheese; remove from heat and cover for 2 minutes to melt.

Serve each patty on a bed of baby spinach leaves, topped with sautéed onions.

Note:

Follow these guidelines to properly cook ground meat using an instant-read meat thermometer:

Beef: 160 degrees and no pink remaining
Turkey: 165 degrees and no pink remaining
Chicken: 165 degrees and no pink remaining
Bison: 160 degrees and no pink remaining

Chapter 3

Dinner

Hearty Main Dish Greek Salad

Delicious and nutritious, this versatile salad can be lightened up by omitting the barley, the chicken or both for a light lunch or side. With these heartier additions, the salad is an ideal one-dish dinner! If you like, you can substitute any whole grain for the barley. **Serves: 6**

Ingredients - Dressing:

2 Tablespoons olive oil (extra-virgin)

1/3 cup red-wine vinegar

1/4 teaspoon pepper (freshly cracked)

1/4 teaspoon salt

6 cloves garlic, minced (or 1 teaspoon garlic powder)

1 teaspoon dried dill (or 1 tablespoon fresh)

Ingredients - Salad:

1 cup cooked and cooled whole barley

2 1/2 cups shredded or chopped cooked chicken

6 cups lettuce (Romaine), coarsely chopped

2 medium fresh tomatoes, chopped

1 large fresh cucumber, peeled, seeded and chopped

1/2 cup feta cheese (crumbled)

1/2 cup red onion, finely chopped

1/4 cup sliced black olives

1/4 cup sliced and pitted Kalamata olives

To Prepare:

In a large bowl, whisk together all dressing ingredients. Add salad ingredients; thoroughly toss to coat with dressing.

Notes:

This recipe is great for using up leftover chicken. If you don't have leftovers, you may poach one pound of chicken breasts.

Barley can take up to 40 minutes to cook; this can be reduced by soaking it overnight.

To make this easy dinner come together in a flash, cook your barley and chicken (if necessary) the night before and refrigerate until you prepare your salad.

Garlic Tofu Stir-Fry

Great for 'meatless Mondays' or any day of the week you want to go vegetarian. **Serves: 4**

Ingredients

2 teaspoons canola oil, divided

1 pound firm tofu, cut into 2-inch strips

1 cup low- or no-sodium chicken broth

4 cloves minced fresh garlic

1 1/2 Tablespoons cornstarch

1/4 teaspoon red pepper flakes, crushed

1 fresh red bell pepper, seeded and sliced into strips

2 cups broccoli (frozen or fresh)

1 can (8 ounces) sliced water chestnuts, drained and rinsed

1 Tablespoon low-sodium soy sauce

1 cup brown rice (optional)

To Prepare:

Cook brown rice as directed on package; keep warm for serving.

Heat a wok or rounded saucepan over medium-high heat; add 1 teaspoon canola oil and stir-fry tofu strips until golden brown. Remove and set aside.

Combine broth, garlic and cornstarch in a small bowl; stir until cornstarch is fully dissolved. Set aside.

Reheat wok. Add remaining teaspoon canola oil, stir-fry pepper strips and broccoli for 1 minute. Add water chestnuts and stir-fry an additional 30 seconds.

Stir cornstarch mixture; add to wok along with tofu and soy sauce. Bring to boiling and cook, stirring occasionally, for 1 to 2 minutes or until slightly thickened.

If desired, serve over brown rice.

Notes:

Any desired protein can be substituted for tofu. Slice into strips and cook as instructed for tofu, until desired degree of doneness is achieved; proceed with following steps.

Vegetable Frittata

Packed with veggies and protein, this versatile dish is as good for dinner as it is for brunch! **Serves: 6**

<u>Ingredients</u>

1 pound asparagus, cut into 1-inch pieces

6 ounces Portobello mushrooms

1 Tablespoon olive oil

2 cloves fresh garlic, minced

1 shallot, minced

1 fresh small zucchini, thinly sliced

6 eggs (large)

1/3 cup milk

1/4 teaspoon salt

Freshly cracked black pepper to taste

1 teaspoon dried chives (or 1 Tablespoon fresh)

Freshly grated nutmeg (optional)

1/4 cup grated Parmesan cheese

1 large fresh tomato, sliced

To Prepare:

Preheat your oven to 350 degrees. Lightly grease a 2-quart casserole (11x7x1.5 inches).

Blanch asparagus by boiling for 1 to 2 minutes, then "shock" by immediately submerging in ice water to preserve color. Drain, dry and set aside.

Wash and slice mushrooms; cook in olive oil over medium heat for approximately 10 minutes or until softened. Add garlic and shallot; cook another 2 minutes. Remove from heat.

Beat together eggs, milk, salt, pepper, nutmeg (if desired) and chives until well combined. Add vegetables to mixture.

Pour mixture into prepared casserole dish and top with sliced tomatoes. Sprinkle cheese over tomatoes. Bake at 350 degrees for 30 to 35 minutes or until golden brown and cooked through. If desired, frittata can be placed under your broiler for 2 to 3 minutes to brown the top.

Cool before serving, serve at room temperature or chilled.

Notes:

Any type of shredded/grated cheese can be substituted for Parmesan.

Chicken-Stuffed Mediterranean Squash

Another ideal option for crisp fall days, this hearty stuffed squash is loaded with good-for-you greens and lean protein.
Serves: 4

Ingredients

2 medium seeded, halved acorn squash

2 Tablespoons plus 1 Teaspoon olive oil (extra-virgin, divided)

1/2 Teaspoon salt, divided

1/2 Teaspoon black pepper (freshly cracked, divided)

1/2 cup onion, finely chopped

2 cloves fresh garlic, minced

2 Tablespoons water

1 Tablespoon tomato paste

1 large bunch Swiss chard, washed and chopped

1 can (15 ounces) white beans, rinsed and drained

1/2 pound ground chicken, cooked and drained

1/4 cup Kalamata olives, pitted and chopped

1/3 cup whole-wheat bread crumbs

1/3 cup grated Parmesan cheese

To Prepare:

Place a rack in the center portion of your oven; preheat your broiler.

Brush the insides of squash with 1 teaspoon olive oil.

Arrange in a microwave-safe 9x13 pan (cut a small slice off the bottom if necessary for balance). Sprinkle on 1/4 teaspoon each salt and pepper; cover with plastic wrap and microwave on high for approximately 10 to 12 minutes, until fork-tender.

While the squash is cooking, heat 1 tablespoon olive oil in a large skillet over medium heat.

Cook and stir onion until it begins to brown, approximately 2 minutes. Add garlic and continue to cook and stir for another minute. Add water, tomato paste, salt and pepper. Add Swiss chard, cover and cook until tender, approximately 3 to 5 minutes. Uncover, add olives and white beans; cook another 3 minutes, stirring occasionally.

Fill each cooked squash half with approximately 1 cup of chard mixture. Stir together Parmesan cheese, breadcrumbs and oil; sprinkle atop filling. Broil stuffed squash halves until topping is browned, approximately 2 minutes.

Note:

Recipe can be made without ground chicken for a hearty vegetarian option.

Greek Chicken Tabbouleh

Traditionally made with processed couscous, this healthier version of tabbouleh includes chicken to transform a side dish into the main event! The bright, light flavors of mint and lemon make this hearty salad ideal for hot summer days. **Serves: 6**

Ingredients

1 3/4 cups water

1 cup quinoa

1 1/2 cups shredded cooked chicken (organic, free-range)

1 medium tomato, seeded and chopped

1/2 cup fresh mint, chopped (or 2 tablespoons dried)

1/4 cup golden raisins

1/4 cup cucumber, chopped

1/4 cup lemon juice, freshly squeezed

2 tablespoons green onions, chopped

1 tablespoon olive oil (extra-virgin)

2 teaspoons green onions, minced

Sea salt and freshly-cracked black pepper to taste

To Prepare:

Cover the quinoa with water; bring to a boil. Reduce heat and simmer, covered, for 20 minutes or until all liquid is absorbed. Fluff with a fork.

Stir in all remaining ingredients, cover and rest for 1 hour. Serve at room temperature or chilled.

Note:

If you don't have leftover chicken, you may poach 1 pound of boneless, skinless chicken breasts for this recipe.

If the flavor of mint is too strong, you may substitute 1/2 cup of fresh, chopped parsley.

Pesto Salmon with Green Beans

Light and flavorful, this recipe incorporates omega-3-packed wild salmon for a delicious warm-weather dinner.
Serves: 4

Ingredients:

1 cup uncooked brown rice

4 cups fresh spinach

1 cup fresh basil

1/2 cup low- or no-sodium chicken broth (homemade if possible)

2 tablespoons extra-virgin olive oil

1/4 teaspoon sea salt

6 cloves fresh garlic, peeled

4 (6 ounce) wild-caught salmon fillets, skinned

1 pound fresh green beans (organic if possible), trimmed and washed

2 tablespoons butter

To Prepare:

Preheat oven to 400 degrees. Lightly grease a shallow baking dish.

Combine brown rice and 2 1/2 cups water in a saucepan. Bring to a boil. Reduce heat and simmer, covered, for 40 to 45 minutes or until rice is tender. Fluff with a fork before serving.

In a blender, combine the first 6 ingredients and process until mixture achieves a smooth consistency.

Spread a thin layer of pesto into the bottom of prepared baking dish. Arrange salmon fillets on top of pesto; spoon remaining pesto over each fillet. Bake for 20 minutes or until fish is opaque in the center and flakes easily when tested with a fork.

While salmon is baking, blanch green beans: bring a large pot of unsalted water to a rolling boil. Submerge beans and cook for 3 minutes. Remove and toss with butter.

Serve each salmon fillet atop 1/3 cup of brown rice with buttered green beans.

Note:

The flavor of fresh green beans is great on its own. If you desire more flavor, feel free to add sea salt and freshly cracked pepper, or any favorite salt-free seasoning blend while tossing with butter.

Chicken – Wild Rice Soup with Roasted Vegetables

Perfect for chilly fall days, this soup highlights the intense flavor of roasted vegetables while swapping healthy wild rice for processed white pasta. For uniform roasting, chop all vegetables into same-size pieces.
Serves: 7

Ingredients

1 cup chopped fresh bell pepper

1 cup chopped fresh celery

1 cup chopped fresh mushrooms

1 cup chopped fresh onion

1 cup chopped fresh carrots

2 tablespoons olive oil (extra virgin)

1 cup water

2 tablespoons fresh rosemary, chopped (or 2 teaspoons dried)

1 tablespoon fresh sage, chopped (or 1 teaspoon dried)

10 cups homemade chicken stock, divided

2 cloves garlic, finely minced

1 pound free-range chicken breast, cut into 1/2-inch pieces

1 cup organic wild rice

To Prepare:

Preheat oven to 375 degrees and line a large baking sheet with foil. Toss chopped vegetables with olive oil; arrange on prepared pan (pieces should not touch) and roast, stirring occasionally, for 50 minutes or until lightly browned.

In a large pot, combine water, rosemary, sage, 7 cups chicken stock, garlic and chicken pieces. Bring to a boil, reduce heat and simmer, uncovered, 30 minutes or until chicken is cooked through. Add roasted vegetables and simmer another 30 minutes.

While the chicken cooks, combine the remaining 3 cups stock and wild rice in a medium saucepan. Bring to a boil, reduce heat and simmer, covered, for approximately 40 minutes or until rice kernels have "puffed" open. Do not overcook, set aside.

Add wild rice to soup and heat through. Serve with whole-grain rolls, if desired.

Note:

If you don't have homemade stock on hand, you may substitute an equal amount of low- or no-sodium chicken broth.

Pizza Casserole

Serves: 6

Ingredients:

3/4 cup coarse barley

1 pound grass-fed ground bison (or any organic, grass-fed ground meat)

8 ounces fresh mushrooms, sliced

1 cup fresh spinach, washed, coarsely chopped

6 medium fresh tomatoes, seeded and chopped

1 1/3 cups no-sugar-added tomato soup

1 clove fresh garlic, minced

1 small onion, minced

1 cup fresh green pepper, chopped

1/4 teaspoon sea salt

Freshly cracked black pepper to taste

1 1/2 teaspoons Italian seasoning blend

1/2 teaspoon red pepper flakes

1 cup shredded mozzarella cheese, divided

1/4 cup grated Parmesan cheese

To Prepare:

In a saucepan, combine barley and 3 cups water. Bring to a boil; reduce heat and simmer, covered, 40 to 50 minutes or until tender but still firm. Set aside.

Preheat oven to 350 degrees and lightly oil or grease a 2-quart baking dish.

In a large skillet over medium heat, cook and stir ground bison and mushrooms until bison is no longer pink and mushrooms are browned. Add spinach and cook for 1 minute to wilt. Drain.

Combine bison mixture, barley, tomatoes, soup, garlic, onion, green pepper, seasonings and 1/2 cup mozzarella cheese.

Bake, uncovered, at 350 degrees for 30 minutes.

During the last 5 minutes of cooking time, sprinkle additional mozzarella and Parmesan cheese over top. If desired, you may place casserole under your broiler after cooking to brown the cheeses, approximately 2 minutes.

Cheesy Chicken-Quinoa Bake

Serves: 6

Ingredients:

1 cup whole quinoa

2 cups homemade chicken stock

3/4 cup fresh red bell pepper, chopped

1 medium red onion, chopped

1 cup crookneck squash, thinly sliced

1 cup organic zucchini, thinly sliced

1 1/2 cups cooked free-range chicken, shredded

1 tablespoon fresh thyme, minced

1 clove garlic, minced

1 cup shredded cheddar or pepper-jack cheese, divided

Freshly cracked black pepper to taste

To Prepare:

Preheat oven to 350 degrees; grease a large baking dish.

Rinse quinoa in water until the water runs clear. Combine the quinoa and stock in a saucepan. Bring to a boil.

Reduce heat and simmer, covered, until all liquid is absorbed, approximately 20 minutes. Fluff with a fork.

Thoroughly combine all ingredients except 1/2 cup cheese in prepared baking dish.

Sprinkle remaining cheese on top and bake, uncovered, for 15 minutes or until heated through.

Note:

Rinsing quinoa is an important step due to the soapy-tasting film on the whole grain.

Taco Skillet

Serves: 6

Ingredients:

1/2 cup brown rice

1 1/4 cups homemade chicken stock

1 teaspoon canola oil

1 medium yellow onion, chopped

1 pound grass-fed ground beef

1/2 teaspoon smoked paprika

1/2 teaspoon cumin

1 teaspoon chili powder

1 clove fresh garlic, minced

1 cup prepared salsa (no sugar added)

10 ounces fresh spinach leaves, washed and patted dry

1/2 cup shredded pepper-jack cheese

1/2 cup plain (unsweetened) Greek yogurt

1 cup chopped avocado

To Prepare:

In a saucepan, combine rice and water. Bring to a boil; reduce heat and simmer, covered, until tender. This can take up to 50 minutes; begin checking your rice at 30 minutes to prevent burning or overcooking.

In a large skillet over medium-high heat, sauté the chopped onion in the canola oil until translucent, approximately 3 minutes.

Add ground beef and seasonings to onion in pan. Cook and stir approximately 10 minutes or until no pink remains. Stir in garlic, salsa and spinach; cook approximately 3 minutes more to wilt spinach. Remove from heat, stir in shredded cheese.

Top each serving with Greek yogurt and chopped avocado, as desired.

Greek Spaghetti Squash

Great for satisfying those pasta cravings, spaghetti squash cooks up remarkably similarly to its refined-carbohydrated alternative!
Serves: 6

Ingredients:

1 large spaghetti squash, cut in half lengthwise, seeded

2 tablespoons canola oil

1 medium red onion, chopped

2 cloves fresh garlic, minced

1 1/2 cups seeded, chopped fresh tomatoes

3 tablespoons pitted and sliced Kalamata olives

3/4 cup crumbled feta cheese

2 tablespoons chopped fresh mint leaves

1 tablespoon chopped fresh dill

To Prepare:

Preheat your oven to 350 degrees; lightly grease baking sheet.

Bake spaghetti squash, cut sides down, for 30 minutes or until done. Squash is done when a sharp knife glides in with little resistance. Set aside until cool enough to handle safely.

In a skillet over medium heat, heat canola oil and sauté onion until soft. Add garlic; cook and stir 2 to 3 minutes; be careful not to burn garlic.

Add tomatoes; heat through.

Scoop the stringy flesh from spaghetti squash. In a large bowl, toss squash with tomato mixture until combined.

Top each serving with feta cheese, mint and dill.

Vegetable-Burger Stir Fry

With better-for-you reduced-sodium soy sauce and a very small amount of added sugar, this quick stir-fry is great for busy weeknights. **Serves: 6**

Ingredients:

1/4 cup homemade chicken stock

1 tablespoon reduced-sodium soy sauce

1 1/2 teaspoons sugar

2 tablespoons freshly squeezed lemon juice

Zest of 1 lemon

3 tablespoons canola oil

1 teaspoon red pepper flakes

2 cups chopped broccoli florets

1 bag (16 ounces) prepared fresh coleslaw mix, rinsed

3 vegetable- or soy-burger patties, cooked as directed on package, crumbled

4 cups cooked brown rice

To Prepare:

In a small bowl, whisk together first 5 ingredients and set aside.

In a wok or large saucepan, heat oil over high heat.

Add the broccoli and red pepper flakes; stir-fry 3 minutes or until crisp-tender.

Add coleslaw mix and soy burger crumbles; toss until heated through and coleslaw mix wilts.

Remove from heat; add prepared sauce and toss thoroughly to coat. Serve over rice.

Note:

In order to make this dinner come together in a flash, cook the brown rice the night before and store, covered tightly, up to 24 hours in the refrigerator and heat in the microwave.

Hearty Steak and Cauliflower "Potatoes"

Sure to satisfy even the most die-hard 'meat and potatoes' lover in your life! **Serves: 4**

Ingredients:

4 (5 ounce) organic, grass-fed top sirloin steaks

1 tablespoon freshly cracked black pepper

1 cup sliced fresh button mushrooms

4 cups cauliflower florets

1/4 cup Parmesan cheese, freshly grated

1 tablespoon cream cheese

1 teaspoon fresh minced garlic

Sea salt and freshly cracked black pepper (to taste)

1 tablespoon fresh chives, chopped

4 tablespoons butter, divided

To Prepare:

Preheat your broiler. Rub steaks with 1 tablespoon pepper. Broil 4 inches from heat for 8 minutes. Turn; broil another 7 to 8 minutes or until steaks have reached desired doneness (see note).

Meanwhile, in a large saucepan, cook cauliflower until very tender, approximately 6 minutes. Dry thoroughly using paper towels. While still hot, place in a food processor with Parmesan cheese, cream cheese, garlic, salt and pepper; process until smooth.

In a skillet, heat 1 tablespoon butter over medium heat. Sauté the mushrooms until golden brown and tender.

Spoon the mushrooms over steaks and serve alongside cauliflower; top each serving of cauliflower with chives and butter.

Note:

Follow these guidelines to perfectly cook your steak using a meat thermometer inserted in the thickest portion of meat:

Medium Rare: 145 degrees
Medium: 160 degrees
Well-Done: 170 degrees

Quick-Cooking Italian Chicken

Serves: 4

Ingredients:

1 cup fresh Roma tomatoes, diced

1/4 cup tablespoons finely diced onion

1/2 cup sliced sweet pimientos, drained

1/2 cup fresh basil leaves, coarsely chopped

1 teaspoon balsamic vinegar

1 1/2 pounds organic, free-range chicken breasts, boneless, skinless

1 tablespoon olive oil

Sea salt and freshly cracked black pepper, to taste

4 cups steamed broccoli

2 cups hot cooked bulgur

To Prepare:

In a bowl, combine tomatoes, onion, pimientos, basil and vinegar; set aside.

Flatten chicken to 1/2 inch thickness between two pieces of foil or waxed paper, using a mallet.

In a skillet over medium-high heat, sauté chicken breasts in olive oil until cooked through and no longer pink, approximately 3 minutes per side.

Serve each chicken breast with tomato mixture spooned over top, alongside, broccoli and bulgur.

Roasted Pork Chop Supper

Serves: 4

Ingredients:

2 tablespoons no-sugar-added apple juice concentrate, thawed

1 tablespoon extra-virgin olive oil

1 tablespoon prepared mustard

1/2 teaspoon sea salt

1/4 teaspoon freshly cracked black pepper

1/2 teaspoon marjoram, dried, crushed

1/4 teaspoon garlic powder

4 organic pork chops, center cut, bone-in, 1/2 inch thick

1 1/2 cups fresh carrots cut into 2-inch pieces

1 medium onion, cut into wedges

2 cups fresh green beans, washed and trimmed

3 cups hot cooked brown rice

To Prepare:

Preheat your oven to 425 degrees. Lightly grease a jelly-roll pan.

In a small bowl, combine first 7 ingredients; set aside.

Toss carrots and onions with half of dressing mixture; set aside. Brush pork chops with remaining dressing mixture; set aside.

Arrange vegetables on prepared pan and roast for 15 minutes.

Add green beans to pan; toss to coat with dressing.

Arrange pork chops on top of vegetable mixture; return to oven and roast for 30 to 40 minutes more, until vegetable are tender and pork chops are done (no pink remains).

Serve with rice and, if desired, whole-grain dinner rolls.

Chicken-Bulgur Florentine

Enjoy the classic flavors of chicken Florentine without the refined carbs of white pasta!

Ingredients:

1 teaspoon canola oil

1 pound organic, free-range chicken breasts, boneless, skinless, cubed

1 clove fresh garlic, minced

10 ounces cream cheese, softened

1 1/2 teaspoons no-sugar-added Italian seasoning blend

3/4 cup milk

2 cups cooked bulgur

1 1/2 pounds fresh spinach leaves, washed and patted dry

1 (15 ounce) can artichoke hearts, drained and chopped

1 cup shredded mozzarella cheese

To Prepare:

Preheat your oven to 375 degrees. Grease a 1 1/2 – or 2-quart baking dish.

In a very large skillet, heat oil over medium heat. Add the chicken and garlic; cook, stirring often, until chicken is no longer pink (approximately 7 minutes). Add all remaining ingredients to skillet, remove from heat and cover until spinach wilts.

Spoon mixture into prepared baking dish. Bake, covered, for 25 minutes or until cheese is melted and dish is heated through. If desired, place under your broiler for 2 to 4 minutes until light golden brown.

Note:

Serve alongside a simple salad of organic baby greens dressed with no-sugar-added Italian dressing.

Herb-Seasoned Tomato-Chicken Barley

Bursting with fresh flavor, this hearty main-dish salad is best served chilled. **Serves: 6**

Ingredients:

1 1/2 teaspoons sugar

1/2 cup rice wine vinegar

1/2 cup sliced red onion

1 large organic cucumber, thinly sliced

4 Roma tomatoes, seeded and chopped

1/4 cup fresh green onions, sliced

1/3 cup fresh basil, chopped

1/3 cup fresh oregano, chopped

2 tablespoons extra-virgin olive oil

1/2 teaspoon crushed red pepper flakes

1 teaspoon sea salt

Freshly cracked black pepper to taste

5 cups hot cooked coarse-kernel barley

3 cups free-range chicken, cooked, shredded or cubed

1/2 cup grated Parmesan cheese

To Prepare:

In a small bowl, combine vinegar and sugar.

Add onion; let stand for 30 minutes.

Drain and reserve 2 tablespoons vinegar mixture.

Combine remaining ingredients, including onion, in a large serving bowl.

Drizzle on reserved vinegar mixture; toss to coat and mix evenly.

Note:

If you prefer, you may sprinkle Parmesan cheese on individual servings.

Serve with a salad of baby greens dressed with no-sugar-added Italian dressing.

Chapter 4

Snacks

Grab-and-Go Tropical Trail Mix

Ideal for avoiding the unhealthy snacks available in most vending machines, this hearty, fiber-packed trail mix is great for kids as well as adults! **Serves: 15 to 20**

Ingredients:

3 cups unsweetened whole-wheat miniature biscuit cereal

1 cup unsweetened banana chips

1 cup unsweetened dried pineapple bits

1 cup dry-roasted macadamia nuts

1 cup pecans, toasted

1 cup unsweetened coconut, toasted

To Prepare:

Thoroughly combine all ingredients; store in an airtight container. Portion out 1/2 cup servings into small plastic zipper bags as needed.

Cajun Spiced Popcorn

Great for groups of hungry kids after school or parties, this spicy, savory popcorn blend serves up big flavor! **Serves: 16**

Ingredients:

16 cups air-popped popcorn (approximately 1/2 cup unpopped kernels)

4 tablespoons butter, melted

1/4 teaspoon red pepper flakes (optional)

1/2 teaspoon cayenne pepper

1/2 teaspoon sea salt

1 teaspoon smoked paprika

1/2 teaspoon garlic powder

1/4 teaspoon freshly cracked black pepper

1/8 teaspoon dried oregano

1/8 teaspoon dried thyme

To Prepare:

Combine butter with seasonings in a small bowl. Drizzle evenly over popcorn and toss or shake to coat.

Southwest Toasted Pepitas

Usually thrown away after Halloween, pumpkin seeds become an easy and healthy snack with minimal effort! **Serves: 8**

Ingredients:

2 cups freshly dried pumpkin seeds (see note)

2 tablespoons canola oil

1/2 teaspoon chili powder

1/2 teaspoon onion powder

1/4 teaspoon ground cumin

1/4 teaspoon ground coriander

1/4 teaspoon dried oregano

1/4 teaspoon dried thyme

1/2 teaspoon garlic powder

1/4 teaspoon cayenne pepper

To Prepare:

Preheat oven to 325 degrees.

Combine canola oil with seasonings in a large bowl; add pepitas and toss to coat evenly.

Spread pepitas in a single layer on a baking sheet.

Roast approximately 45 minutes, stirring every 15 minutes, until golden brown and crisp.

Note:

To dry fresh pumpkin seeds, remove all pulp and rinse under cold running water.

Spread in a single layer on a baking sheet and let the pepitas dry for 24 hours.

Savory Stuffed Mushrooms

Serves: 20

Ingredients:

2 pounds button mushrooms, washed, stems removed, chopped and set aside

6 tablespoons butter

8 ounces cream cheese, at room temperature

1/2 cup grated Parmesan cheese

2 tablespoons chopped fresh chives

1/4 teaspoon garlic powder

To Prepare:

Preheat broiler.

In a skillet over medium heat, sauté half the mushroom caps in 3 tablespoons butter until browned.

Drain and repeat with remaining mushroom caps and butter.

In a bowl, combine remaining ingredients including chopped mushroom stems; spoon into mushroom caps.

Arrange on baking sheet and broil approximately 4 minutes or until golden brown.

Classic Buffalo Wings

Reimagined without unhealthy trans-fat frying, these hot-and-spicy chicken wings are perfect for parties! **Serves 4**

Ingredients:

1 pound chicken wings

1 1/2 teaspoons salt

1 tablespoon cayenne pepper

1 teaspoon red pepper flakes

1 teaspoon freshly cracked black pepper

1/4 cup hot sauce (no sugar added)

1 tablespoon butter, melted

To Prepare:

Preheat broiler; grease a 13x9 inch baking dish.

In a large saucepan, combine chicken, salt, cayenne, red pepper flakes and black pepper. Cover with water and bring to a boil. Boil for 15 minutes or until cooked through.

Place wings in baking dish. Broil for 15 to 20 minutes or until desired crispness is reached.

Combine the hot sauce and butter in a bowl; add broiled wings and toss to coat. Serve immediately.

Note:

For a classic presentation, serve these spicy wings with homemade or purchased (no-sugar-added) blue cheese dressing and fresh celery sticks.

Creamy Deviled Eggs

Instead of mayonnaise, these delicious eggs use cream cheese and Cajun spices for a hearty, spicy kick of flavor. For kids or for those who prefer things with less spice, reduce seasonings as desired.
Serves: 24

Work/Total Time: 10 minutes

Ingredients:

12 cage-free eggs, hard-boiled, peeled

1/8 teaspoon dried thyme

1/8 teaspoon dried oregano

1/4 teaspoon smoked paprika, plus more for garnish

Freshly cracked black pepper

1/8 teaspoon garlic powder

1/8 teaspoon cayenne pepper

1/8 teaspoon onion powder

1 1/2 tablespoons sweet pickle relish

1/2 cup cream cheese, softened

1/4 cup plain unsweetened Greek yogurt (optional)

To Prepare:

Halve eggs; carefully scoop out yolks and place in a small bowl.

Using a fork, mash remaining ingredients until smooth. If needed, add yogurt, 1 tablespoon at a time, to reach desired consistency.

Pipe or spoon mixture back into white portions of eggs. Garnish with a sprinkling of paprika.

Refrigerate until ready to serve.

Coco-Nutty Banana Bites

Sure to entice even picky eaters, these sugar-free banana treats are something the whole family will enjoy!

Serves: 4

Ingredients:

2 bananas, sliced diagonally into 2-inch pieces

1/4 cup natural nut butter (cashew, almond, macadamia)

4 teaspoons shredded coconut, toasted, unsweetened

Unsweetened cocoa powder for garnish

For each banana bite, spread approximately 1 teaspoon nut butter on a flat side. Press or sprinkle coconut over the nut butter. Sprinkle a small amount of cocoa powder over the coconut.

Notes:

Natural nut butters should contain only two ingredients – nuts and salt.

If you find traditional unsweetened cocoa powder too bitter, try unsweetened Dutch process cocoa powder. This variety has been processed to remove its acidity, allowing more naturally sweet cocoa flavor to shine through.

Chapter 5

Additional Resources

Other Popular Best Selling Cookbooks For Kindle and Print

We have listed both the short titles and the full titles of these books to make them easier to locate.

You can also search Amazon.com for "best selling cookbooks 2012" or "best selling cookbooks 2013" for an up to date listing.

Other Titles by New Health CookBooks

My Virgin Diet CookBook: The Gluten-Free, Soy-Free, Egg-Free, Dairy-Free, Peanut-Free, Corn-Free and Sugar-Free Cookbook by Rebecca Lorraine

My Fast Metabolism Diet Cookbook: The Wheat-Free, Soy-Free, Dairy-Free, Corn-Free & Sugar-Free Cookbook by New Health CookBooks

It Starts With Food CookBook: The Low Sugar Gluten-Free & Whole Food CookBook - 40 Delicious & Healthy Recipes Your Family Will Love by New Health Cookbooks

Cookbooks by Other Authors

Cooking Light Cookbook by Cooking Light

Cooking Light The Essential Dinner Tonight Cookbook: Over 350 Delicious, Easy, and Healthy Meals by Cooking Light

Forks Over Knives Cookbook by Del Sroufe

Forks Over Knives-The Cookbook: Over 300 Recipes for Plant-Based Eating All Through the Year by Del Sroufe

The Low Blood Sugar Cookbook by Patricia Krimmel, Edward Krimmel

The Low Blood Sugar Cookbook: Sugarless Cooking for Everyone by Patricia Krimmel, Edward Krimmel

The Blood Sugar Solution Cookbook by Mark Hyman

The Blood Sugar Solution Cookbook: More than 175 Ultra-Tasty Recipes for Total Health and Weight Loss by Mark Hyman

Eat What You Love by Marlene Koch

Eat What You Love: More than 300 Incredible Recipes Low in Sugar, Fat, and Calories by Marlene Koch

From Mama's Table to Mine by Bobby Deen

From Mama's Table to Mine: Everybody's Favorite Comfort Foods at 350 Calories or Less by Bobby Deen

Gather, the Art of Paleo Entertaining by Bill Staley and Hayley Mason

It's All Good by Gwyneth Paltrow

It's All Good: Delicious, Easy Recipes That Will Make You Look Good and Feel Great by Gwyneth Paltrow

Jumpstart to Skinny: The Simple 3-Week Plan for Supercharged Weight Loss by Bob Harper and Greg Critser

My Beef with Meat by Rip Esselstyn

My Beef with Meat: The Healthiest Argument for Eating a Plant-Strong Diet--Plus 140 New Engine 2 Recipes by Rip Esselstyn

Nourishing Traditions by Sally Fallon

Nourishing Traditions: The Cookbook that Challenges Politically Correct Nutrition and the Diet Dictocrats by Sally Fallon

Practical Paleo by Diane Sanfilippo

Practical Paleo: A Customized Approach to Health and a Whole-Foods Lifestyle by Diane Sanfilippo

Primal Blueprint Quick and Easy Meals by Mark Sisson and Jennifer Meier

Primal Blueprint Quick and Easy Meals: Delicious, Primal-approved meals you can make in under 30 minutes by Mark Sisson and Jennifer Meier

Relish by Daphne Oz

Relish: An Adventure in Food, Style, and Everyday Fun by Daphne Oz

Superfood Smoothies by Julie Morris

Superfood Smoothies: 100 Delicious, Energizing & Nutrient-dense Recipes by Julie Morris

The America's Test Kitchen Healthy Family Cookbook by America's Test Kitchen

The America's Test Kitchen Healthy Family Cookbook: A New, Healthier Way to Cook Everything from America's Most Trusted Test Kitchen by America's Test Kitchen

The Biggest Loser Cookbook by Devin Alexander and Karen Kaplan

The Biggest Loser Cookbook: More Than 125 Healthy, Delicious Recipes Adapted from NBC's Hit Show by Devin Alexander and Karen Kaplan

The Fresh 20 by Melissa Lanz

The Fresh 20: 20-Ingredient Meal Plans for Health and Happiness 5 Nights a Week by Melissa Lanz

The Mediterranean Diet Cookbook by Rockridge University Press

The Mediterranean Diet Cookbook: A Mediterranean Cookbook with 150 Healthy Mediterranean Diet Recipes by Rockridge University Press

The Paleo Diet Cookbook by Loren Cordain and Nell Stephenson

The Paleo Diet Cookbook: More Than 150 Recipes for

Paleo Breakfasts, Lunches, Dinners, Snacks, and Beverages by Loren Cordain and Nell Stephenson

What's for Dinner? by Curtis Stone

What's for Dinner?: Delicious Recipes for a Busy Life by Curtis Stone

Wheat Belly Cookbook by William Davis MD

Wheat Belly Cookbook: 150 Recipes to Help You Lose the Wheat, Lose the Weight, and Find Your Path Back to Health by William Davis MD

Weight Loss Books And Diet Books

You can also search for "weight loss books best sellers 2012" or "weight loss best sellers 2013" for a current list.

The Atkins Diet

Dr. Atkins' New Diet Revolution by Robert C. Atkins

Cooked by Michael Pollan

Cooked: A Natural History of Transformation by Michael Pollan

Eat to Live by Joel Fuhrman

Eat to Live: The Amazing Nutrient-Rich Program for Fast and Sustained Weight Loss by Joel Fuhrman

Fat Chance by Robert H. Lustig

Fat Chance: Beating the Odds Against Sugar, Processed Food, Obesity, and Disease by Robert H. Lustig

Fat Chance Cookbook by Robert H. Lustig, Heather Milar, & Cindy Gershen

The Fat Chance Cookbook: More Than 100 Recipes Ready in Under 30 Minutes to Help You Lose the Sugar and the Weight by Robert H. Lustig, Heather Milar, Cindy Gershen

Good Calories, Bad Calories by Gary Taubes

The Blood Sugar Solution by Mark Hyman

The Blood Sugar Solution: The UltraHealthy Program for Losing Weight, Preventing Disease, and Feeling Great Now! by Mark Hyman

The 5:2 Diet Book by Kate Harrison

The 5:2 Diet Book: Feast for 5 Days a Week and Fast for 2 to Lose Weight, Boost Your Brain and Transform Your Health by Kate Harrison

The Five Two Diet Book

The Art and Science of Low Carbohydrate Living by Stephen Phinney and Jeff Volek

The Art and Science of Low Carbohydrate Living: An Expert Guide to Making the Life-Saving Benefits of Carbohydrate Restriction Sustainable and Enjoyable by

Stephen Phinney, Jeff Volek

The Fast Diet by Michael Mosley and Mimi Spencer

The Fast Diet: Lose Weight, Stay Healthy, and Live Longer with the Simple Secret of Intermittent Fasting by Michael Mosley and Mimi Spencer

The Fast Metabolism Diet by Haylie Pomroy

The Fast Metabolism Diet: Eat More Food and Lose More Weight by Haylie Pomroy

The New Atkins for a New You by Dr. Eric C. Westman, Dr. Stephen D. Phinney, Jeff S. Volek

The Paleo Solution by Robb Wolf

The Paleo Solution: The Original Human Diet by Robb Wolf, or Rob Wolf
Wheat Belly by William Davis MD

Wheat Belly: Lose the Wheat, Lose the Weight, and Find Your Path Back To Health by William Davis MD

The Primal Blueprint by Mark Sisson

The Primal Blueprint: Reprogram your genes for effortless weight loss, vibrant health and boundless energy by Mark Sisson

The Healthy Green Drink Diet by Jason Manheim

The Healthy Green Drink Diet: Advice and Recipes to

Energize, Alkalize, Lose Weight, and Feel Great by Jason Manheim

Forks Over Knives by Gene Stone

Forks Over Knives: The Plant-Based Way to Health by Gene Stone

Deadly Harvest by Geoff Bond

Deadly Harvest: The Intimate Relationship Between Our Heath and Our Food by Geoff Bond

The Rosedale Diet by Ron Rosedale and Carol Colman

Ignore the awkward by Uffe Ravnskov

Ignore the awkward! How the cholesterol myths are kept alive by Uffe Ravnskov

Primal Body, Primal Mind by Nora Gedgaudas

Primal Body, Primal Mind: Beyond the Paleo Diet for Total Health and a Longer Life by Nora T. Gedgaudas, CNS, CNT

Deep Nutrition by Catherine Shanahan

Deep Nutrition: Why Your Genes Need Traditional Food by Catherine Shanahan MD

The Skinny Rules by Bob Harper

The Skinny Rules: The Simple, Nonnegotiable Principles for Getting to Thin by Bob Harper

Protein Power by Dr. Eades

Protein Power: The High-Protein/Low-Carbohydrate Way to Lose Weight, Feel Fit, and Boost Your Health--in Just Weeks! by Michael R. Eades, Mary Dan Eades

Eat to Live by Dr. Joel Fuhrman

Eat to Live: The Amazing Nutrient-Rich Program for Fast and Sustained Weight Loss by Joel Fuhrman

The Paleo Answer by Loren Cordain

The Paleo Answer: 7 Days to Lose Weight, Feel Great, Stay Young by Loren Cordain

The Seventeen Day Diet by Mike Moreno

The 17 Day Diet by Mike Moreno

The China Study by T. Colin Campbell

The China Study: The Most Comprehensive Study of Nutrition Ever Conducted And the Startling Implications for Diet by T. Colin Campbell

Choose to Lose by Chris Powell

Choose to Lose: The 7-Day Carb Cycle Solution by Chris Powell

Fit2Fat2Fit by Drew Manning

Fit2Fat2Fit: The Unexpected Lessons from Gaining and Losing 75 lbs on Purpose by Drew Manning

The Belly Fat Diet by John Chatham

The Belly Fat Diet: Lose Your Belly, Shed Excess Weight, Improve Health by John Chatham

The Dukan Diet Book by Pierre Dukan

The Dukan Diet: 2 Steps to Lose the Weight, 2 Steps to Keep It Off Forever by Pierre Dukan

The Mayo Clinic Diet Book

The Mayo Clinic Diet: Eat Well, Enjoy Life, Lose Weight by Mayo Clinic

The Mayo Clinic Diabetes Diet by Mayo Clinic

The Virgin Diet by JJ Virgin

The Virgin Diet: Drop 7 Foods, Lose 7 Pounds, Just 7 Days by JJ Virgin

101 Best Foods to Boost Your Metabolism by Metabolic-Calculator.com

Pure Fat Burning Fuel by Isabel De Los Rios

Pure Fat Burning Fuel: Follow This Simple, Heart Healthy Path To Total Fat Loss by Isabel De Los Rios

It Starts with Food by Dallas & Melissa Hartwig

It Starts with Food: Discover the Whole30 and Change Your Life in Unexpected Ways - Dallas & Melissa Hartwig

Shred by Ian K. Smith

Shred: The Revolutionary Diet: 6 Weeks 4 Inches 2 Sizes by Ian K. Smith

The Four Hour Body by Timothy Ferriss

The 4-Hour Body: The Secrets and Science of Rapid Body Transformation by Timothy Ferriss

VB6 by Mark Bittman

VB6: Eat Vegan Before 6:00 to Lose Weight and Restore Your Health . . . for Good by Mark Bittman

VB6: Eat Vegan Before 6:00 to Lose Weight and Restore Your Health . . . for Good by Mark Bittman

Wheat Belly by William Davis MD

Wheat Belly: Lose the Wheat, Lose the Weight, and Find Your Path Back To Health by William Davis MD

Why We Get Fat by Gary Taubes

Why We Get Fat: And What to Do About It by Gary Taubes

CPSIA information can be obtained at www.ICGtesting.com
Printed in the USA
LVOW01s1528181015

458752LV00031B/1665/P

9 781493 575794